870 S

Startups and Money Making Ideas

Including 54 reasons you should start today, a step by step process to getting started, tips for success, plus free online resources for the frugal new business owner

By Sara Martin

Table of Contents

4

Disclaimer

This book is for informational purposes only and is not meant to take the place of a business mentor or attorney. Before starting or running any of the business in this book or from elsewhere, we recommend that you consult with and show your ideas/ plans to a business attorney for legal advice so you can be knowledgeable of the laws in your jurisdiction pertaining to your particular business. By using any of the information in this book, you free the author and/or publisher from any liability. You use any and all of the information, ideas, businesses, sources, websites listed or any of the information in this book at your own risk. Any third party also uses any of the information in this book or does business with you at their own risk. I the author and the publisher are not responsible for anything that results from you or anyone using any of the information in this book, any acts of nature, loss of money, loss of investments, acts of God, anything situational of yours or a third party, loss of property, destruction of property, physical injury/ harm or bodily injury of anyone, or acts from others that result from you or anyone using any of the information contained in this book. Everything you do from information you read about in this book, you do by your own risk. Everything you do is through your own judgment; any situation you put yourself in is through your own accord and at your own risk. You begin and operate any of these businesses, clubs, societies, groups, organizations, or services or anything not mentioned above at your own risk. It is recommended that you do additional research to fill in holes of knowledge in the business that you decide to startup before getting started. You are responsible to be knowledgeable of and to obtain any necessary insurance, education, degrees, certificates, and/ or certification necessary to run any business listed according to the laws and requirements of the location of your residence and/ or business.

I the author and the publisher are not affiliated with any of the websites or businesses mentioned in this book. You use any of their services at your own risk. Any third party also uses any of the resources in this book at their own risk. This book is purely for encouragement and informational purposes only and it is recommended that you obtain any legal advice from a fully licensed/ credentialed business attorney in your state. This book is not in any way considered legal counsel or business advice. Research any company, person, or situation you wish to do business with or become involved with beforehand, even the ones in this book. You deal with every company (including but not limited to the ones in this book), any person, and any situation at your own risk. It is also your own responsibility that you obtain correct and appropriate permits, licenses, zoning permission/ permits, tax percentages, tax forms, legal help, insurance, background checks, people, and anything else you may need to run your business honestly, ethically and legally.

Some steps to starting your business may not be mentioned in this book. It is your responsibility to seek the advice of a business attorney to make sure you have followed all necessary steps pertaining to your particular business in your particular area. The author and/or publisher is in no way responsible for anything

Welcome to this great opportunity of owning your own business!

You can feel and be successful in life by starting and creating a money making business. You have already taken the first step to achieving a high quality of life. That first step is having the interest and desire to start a business of your own. You have also already taken the second step to owning your own successful business by merely purchasing this valuable book. I bet you didn't even know you had two steps completed! In this book you will find 860 startup businesses and money making ideas. Many of these businesses you could start for less than 100 dollars (not including possible business permits and/or licenses). You are bound to find one that will catch your eye and change your life. But first I will motivate you. I will share with you many amazing and life changing reasons to start your own business. You will be excited to get started!

Some of these reasons may be the reason you would like to go into business for yourself, some may not. Yet you will benefit from all these reasons. Some are economy related, some are health related, and others are freedom, enjoyment, pride, social, community, dream achievement, family, or skill related. Your particular reason may be your key factor, but you will discover that you may benefit in ways you didn't even know of before this reading. You may even find yourself rereading through these next several pages for extra motivation as you discover your favorite business, and move through the steps to starting your business. Continually you may find yourself rereading these reasons after you start your business. These reasons may be forever motivating to you as you run your business on a daily basis. With hard work and perseverance for these reasons, you will stay motivated and may see your life transform before your very eyes.

It is my hope that you will run your business honestly and respectfully. Always keep your constant liability in mind. For example, health and cleanliness is the major concern in food related businesses. 100% supervision and safety is the major concern in child minding and care related businesses. Prepare for the worst, but expect the best. Always run your business to the highest of standards so that all customers and clients may feel highly confident and satisfied with your product or service. Besides not wanting any lawsuits or angry customers, you want them to come back for future business and to pay you again. In most businesses, repeat customers will bring in a large percentage of your revenue.

Step three you will have finished by the time you complete the reading of this book. Step three is actually doing the research necessary in order to find out what business fits you best. To begin with, you will need to figure out which of these questions sounds the most appealing. Will I sell something? Will I provide a service? Will I be organizing group activities? Or will I be entertaining? We have done years of research for you. This book contains 870 options. There has never before been a book with this many ideas! There has never before been a book that has made the process of finding out what business fits best for you so simple!

After you have decided what kind of business you wish to start and feel you are ready to get started, you can move on to step four. Step four is to obtain the necessary permit(s), certification(s), license(s), and legal information necessary to start your business of choice in your community. Do not take this step as a hurdle to starting your own business, as it is really quite simple. Merely check with your local/ community (home owner association, if applicable, etc), town/city, county, state, and federal government websites for information on their rules and requirements to start your business of choice. This book is written primarily for US audiences, but if you are in another country merely work up in levels from your community government to your Federal Government in terms of following rules and regulations). If you have any questions then call, make an appointment to meet with, or email the community or government agencies necessary to answer your questions and concerns. To obtain these numbers, look online on their official websites.

No laws or legal information will be covered in this book. This book is not a source of legal advice. Each community, town/city, county, state and country has different laws pertaining to regulations, permits, insurance issues, safety regulations, zoning issues, and more and you will need to know these to run your business safely and at minimum liability. It is your responsibility as a potential business owner to check your local laws and requirements all the way up to Federal laws pertaining to your business before attempting to get started. After you have researched this information, consult a business attorney to make sure you are not forgetting anything and that you are aware of all the laws and requirements in your jurisdiction relating to your business. Bring in your business plan and don't forget to also discuss procedures, taxes, zoning, liability and insurance. It is best to consult the business attorney after researching as you will not have to pay the attorney for extra time and additional research for things you can find easily online.

Lastly, I want to encourage you to continue to follow your dreams whether the road seems easy, if your business goes through some hard times, or if it is slow to start. Slow beginnings are common as you get the word out and gather a regular client base. Don't give up if you truly believe in your business and your heart is in it. Many times only a change in advertising methods or a small change in the way things are being run is all that is needed to bring a seemingly unsuccessful business into money making mode.

Low start-up costs make it possible for almost anyone to start many of these businesses. No matter what your budget, there is a business for you. Starting a business of one's own has long been the American dream. Our great-grandparents all around the world once operated their own businesses. They sold fruit from roadside stands, opened up small stores in small towns, sold their wears in big city markets, and much more. Many people believe that the ability for one to start their own business is no longer available to the average first world citizen because of the present day success of large corporations. Fortunately this is not so, you also have the opportunity to open up your own business. There are many holes that large corporations have not yet filled or will never be able to fill. Starting a small business is still very possible today in America and in most of the world. It is a great way to work towards living the American Dream of independence, comfort and wealth. This dream is nearly universal the world over. Most large corporations today were started as mom and pop restaurants or home based ideas. They have a lot in common with many of the businesses contained in this book. There is no limit to how far you can take your business or organization. Don't quit your day job yet. But in your spare time, get started! You can soon be a business owner. Welcome to the beginning of your journey, prepare for limitless opportunities.

Reasons to start your own business

Health Related Reasons to Start Your Own Business

1. Your current job brings you anxiety or makes you physically ill.
2. You do not want stress about deadlines from a boss or overhead supervisor.
3. You currently have (or in the future may have) a health condition that makes holding a traditional job with regular 9-5 hours difficult.
4. You currently have (or in the future have) a health condition that makes commuting to a workplace difficult.
5. You want to have control of your work environment in the aspect that you do not want to be exposed to any hazards or toxins.
6. You do not enjoy being micromanaged or to have oversight from superiors.

Family Related Reasons to Start Your Own Business

7. You want/ need time flexibility without the added emotional stress. When you need to take off for doctor's appointments, sick kids at home, etc. you will have no worry as to what your superiors will be thinking.
8. You would like to include your family, friends and/or kids in your business.
9. You want to create a legacy for future generations of your family or those you care about.
10. You may not need childcare if you work at home. Childcare can be very expensive and you could miss out on many of your child's special milestones.
11. You will be able to take your kids to your job with you and not worry about what your superiors would think.
12. You want to bring about a lifestyle related change for yourself and/or your family.

Dream Related Reasons to Start Your Own Business

13. Starting your own business can be a new beginning full of great possibilities.
14. You imagine quitting your current job someday.

15. You have a dream you would like to follow that is not possible with your current job or with working for someone else.

Economy Related Reasons to Start Your Own Business

16. The economy is always in flux, you do not want to worry about layoffs.
17. Jobs may be scarce at your location or in your field.
18. College is very expensive and costs are only rising.
19. The last 5 years have lessened the competition because of a bad economy (at the time of this publication).
20. You want to help others. You'll be contributing to the economy and not taking another job. You will create jobs.

Money Related Reasons to Start Your Own Business

21. You want a salary of limitless possibility.
22. If you work from home you may not need to invest in work clothes.
23. You can start a business with very little investment and the returns can be large.
24. Tax benefits! Vacation, some of your home mortgage, and more can become business tax write-offs.
25. You enjoy not just gambling, but building.

Using Your Skills Related Reasons to Start Your Own Business

26. You feel you can do something better than another business.
27. You have skills you cannot profit from currently.
28. You have skills that you want to contribute to society but that you currently have no outlet for.
29. You don't have many employable skills and have been out of the job market for awhile.
30. You have many great ideas and are not able to use them in your current job situation.
31. You are a hard worker and are self motivated.

Community/ Social Related Reasons to Start Your Own Business

32. You would like a higher status in your community/ personal life. Being a business owner equals societal prestige.
33. You would like to fulfill a need in your community.

34. You like the idea that there is a possibility of great personal fame.
35. You want to bring about change in your community.
36. You want to influence a large number of people.
37. You like to plan events and get people together.
38. You can hire your own people or work alone. You have a good chance of avoiding personality clashes.

Enjoyment/ Pride Related Reasons to Start Your Own Business

39. You can do what you love and love what you do.
40. You can take the greatest pride in your work knowing you are investing in yourself and your own business.
41. You will likely feel much more motivated knowing you are working for yourself and your own business, not just for a paycheck.
42. You have lots of creative energy and currently have no outlet. You're a creative person.
43. You can turn your interests and/or hobbies into money.
44. You feel like a robot at your current job.
45. You want to feel a sense of personal empowerment if you currently feel stuck in your job.
46. You want to feel a sense of personal empowerment in your job if you currently have no/ low income.

Freedom Related Reasons to Start Your Own Business

47. You want to live in the middle or nowhere or anywhere you want and do not want to be tied to a location because of a job.
48. You do not want to commute to work and would prefer to work in the comfort of your own home.
49. You want to set your own hours and do not enjoy someone else making your schedule. Maybe you like to sleep in every day.
50. You are a stay at home mom or a college student and need to have a flexible schedule based around your class schedule or when your child's other parent is home.
51. You like to be the decision maker and do not like being told what to do.

52. You are a retiree and want to only have as many hours as you feel up to during each week.
53. You can incorporate some businesses with your love of travel.
54. You can run some businesses while traveling and can stay longer and/or travel further if you can make money on the internet.

Step by Step Process for Starting Your Own Business

(This is a general overview and there may be more, check with a business attorney, your home owners association (if applicable), local, city, county, state, and federal government to make sure you have all bases covered from their standpoint before getting started)

1. Go through the lists of businesses in this book and list on a separate piece of paper in a column all of the businesses that are related to your interests, skills, current hobbies, and positive experiences. Try to list at least 20
2. Narrow the list down to 15 by crossing out 5 that may require you to take out loans for you to start up or may be more expensive to start up than you are comfortable with.
3. Next narrow it down to 10 by crossing out 5 that may not have clientele for your operating area, and then narrow it down to 5.
4. Consider ethics and how comfortable you would be running these types of businesses and narrow down your list to top 3 by crossing off two more.
5. Consider your interests, skills (or ability to get the necessary skills for these businesses) to narrow down to the top one.
6. Create a business plan (visit http://www.sba.gov to learn how)
7. Research and apply to possible government grant programs (do not have to be paid back), loans (will have to be paid back), and investors. Especially research possible government grant programs. Many are aimed at women, minorities, and the disabled who want to start a small business. However, there could be some related to geographic area or any other specific subject.
8. Check with different government levels considering community, city, county, state and federal permits/licenses you may need. Check with local zoning laws, insurance requirements/ needs (if applicable).
9. Consult a business attorney to make sure you have all legal issues covered.
10. Find suppliers, create products (if applicable), set-up restaurant, store, or other business. At this time also pick

your favorite and most appropriate advertising options within your startup budget. Stay tuned for our second book that will give you over 230 advertising options. Start with 3 and expand to include more later.

11. Build and publish a website. Consider selling online if you have a product or a service.

12. Grand Opening! Celebrate with a big event. Don't forget to advertise and promote heavily beforehand for this event.

Pick Your New Business Now

This is where it gets fun! There are literally hundreds of money making ideas to choose from here.

Publishing/ Research/ Writing/ Printing

1. Web design/ Consulting
2. Web Site Creation (making sites such as a book swapping or social networking)
3. E-commerce Website Publishing
4. Online Auction Site Creation
5. Editing Service/ Proofreading
6. Online Pet Adoption Website
7. Magazine Publishing (kids, teens, women, religious, etc)
8. Book Publishing
   - Poetry
   - Fiction
   - Non Fiction
     - How to Books
     - Local History
     - Children's Books
     - Hobby or Skill Books
     - Relaxation Guides
     - Cook Books
     - Course Books
9. Restaurant and Menu Creation Publishing
10. Independent Music Label
11. Desk Top Publishing/ News Letter Creation (free local to international, advertising for revenue)
12. Mailing Service (sell advertising)
13. Resume Preparation Service
14. Fact Researcher for Academics
15. Typing Service
16. Calligrapher
17. Infopreneur and/or selling affiliate products on your website
18. Freelance writing for Magazines, publishers (buy source book titled: Writer's Market)
19. Handwriting Analysis Consultant
20. Membership Web Site

- Provide Ideas
- Provide Community/ friendship
- Provide Support
- Provide Special Events
- Recommend Products from Affiliates
- Provide Lots of Relevant Information

21. Club Website (with dues paid online)
22. Correspondence Courses or an Online School (example of things to include: newsletters, competitions, certificates of completion, etc)
23. Association Website
24. Social Media Management/ Marketing Business
25. Online News site (local to international, sell advertising)
26. Speech Writing Service
27. Become a Freelance Biographer
28. Freelance Copywriter
29. Invitation Printing
30. Lamination Service
31. Ghostwriting Business
32. Handwriting Service (letters, advertising, invitations, etc)
33. Social Network Game Creator/ Designer
34. Phone App Creator
35. Typing/ Word Processing Business

Parties/ Performing/ Entertainment/ Events

36. Grand Opening Service
37. Children's Party Planning Service
38. Party Planning Service for Adults
39. Reunion Coordinator
40. Entertainer for Children's Parties (clown, mime, magician, princess, juggler)
41. Singer (for parties, events, and/or weddings)
42. Dancer (for parties or events)
43. Musician (harpist, violin player, for weddings, etc)
44. Direct selling of merchandise at home parties
45. Event Planning Service
46. Teach Crafts/ Skills at Parties (example pre-teen party, jewelry making)
47. Balloon Delivery Service
48. Foreign Language Class/ Theme Party
49. DJ for parties/events
50. Host Beauty Pageants/ Start Your Own Pageants
51. Fortune Teller at your own site and/or for parties (palm reader, numerology, tarot card reader, tea leaf reader, crystal ball readings, astrology, psychic)
52. Wedding Photographer
53. Event Photographer (graduation photos, engagement photos, baby photos)
54. Christmas/ Gift Buying and Wrapping Service
55. Holiday Party Service
56. Event Host Location
57. Street Performer
58. Motivational Speaker (and sell personally written relevant books to make more money at events)
59. Ordained Minister (perform weddings, funerals, have own location/ chapel, or travel out locally)
60. Singing Telegram Service
61. Multimedia Presentation Service/ Videographer (make Power Point presentations, videos)
62. Mobile Art Gallery (with parties/events to attract patrons)
63. Start a 800# or 900# (psychic readings, etc., get mechanism to accept credit cards)
64. Face Painting Clown at Carnivals/ Fairs/ On the Street

65. Wedding Planner
66. Ventriloquist Performer
67. Start a Recording Studio
68. Arcade
69. Traveling Theater
70. Puppet Shows/ Marionette or Hand Puppets (parties or events)
71. Modeling Agency
72. Start a Game Competition (charge entry fees, fees for people playing, hire sponsors)
73. Image Consultant
74. Haunted House (seasonal)
75. Carnival, Fair, or Festival (music, cultural, holiday, etc)
76. VHS to DVD Conversion Service/ Cassette to CD Conversion Service/ 8 Track to CD Conversion Service/ Old Video Projector Reel to DVD Service
77. Comedy/ Club Act
78. A Performing Arts Theater
79. Headshot/ Portfolio Photographer
80. Society (historical, cultural, activity related, etc)
81. Roller Skating Rink/ Ice Skating Rink
82. Miniature Golf Course
83. Night Club/ Dance Hall
84. Opera Company
85. Supervised Teen Hangout (Lounge, Sports, Paddle Tennis, Ping Pong)
86. Party Games Hosting
87. Pony Rides for Kids
88. Portable Stages and Platform Rental
89. Record Label and Promo
90. Square Dance Caller/ Club
91. Talent Casting Agency
92. Wedding Centerpieces Creation
93. Animals for Parties/ Petting Zoo
94. Laser Tag Parties
95. Murder Mystery Parties
96. Dove Releases
97. Sward Swallower for Parties/ Events
98. Juggler for Parties/ Events

99. Fire Dancer for Parties/ Events
100. Circus Acts for Parties/ Events
- Trapeze Acts
- Unicycle
- Contortionist
- Plate Spinner
101. Hypnotist
102. Illusionist/ Magician
103. Celebrity Impersonator
104. Origami Instruction Parties
105. Tea Parties
106. Santa Claus Impersonations/ Appearances
107. Artist/ Talent Promoter

Hospitality/ Home/ Office Maintenance

108. Neighborhood Welcoming Service
109. House Cleaning/ Maid Service
110. Window Washing Service
111. Landscaping Design/ Install Contractor
112. Room Painting/ House Painting Service
113. Curb Painting Service (go door to door and paint house numbers on curbs)
114. Swimming Pool Maintenance Service
115. Organizational/ Minimal Living Service/ Clutter Consultant
116. Feung Shui Consultant
117. Laundry/ Cleaning Pick Up Delivery Service
118. Packing, Moving, and/or Unpacking Service
119. Carpet Cleaning Service
120. Handy Man Service
121. Mini Blinds Cleaning/ Install/ Repair Service
122. Personal Chef/ In-home Cook and Clean Up Service
123. House-sitting Service
124. Firewood Delivery
125. Upholstery Cleaning Service
126. Christmas Lights Installation Service (seasonal)
127. Backyard Farming/Agriculture (higher cost foods: mushrooms, sprouts, blueberries, etc)
128. Backyard Earthworm Farming
129. Romantic Night In Service (supply candles, decorations, food)
130. Restaurant Food Delivery Service
131. Lock Smith/ Key making
132. Pet Door Installation Service
133. Home Inspection/ Building Inspector
134. Wall Paper Installation Business
135. HVAC Technician (you can study at home from pennfoster.edu)
136. Furniture Refurbishing
137. Alterations Business
138. Leaflet Distribution Service Business
139. Pick Up Mail/ Feed Pets/ Take Out Trash etc. Service (For Out of Town Clients)
140. Grocery Delivery Service

141. Nursery (Plant)
142. Plumbing
143. Snow Removal Service (seasonal)
144. Ceramic Tile Installation/ Hardwood Floor Installation
145. Pest Control/ Termite Control Elimination Business
146. Home Gutter Cleaning/ Chimney Sweep Business
147. Home Pressure Washing Business
148. Realtor
149. Real Estate Appraisal Business
150. Leaf Raking Business (seasonal)
151. Yard Maintenance Business
152. Home Theater Installation/ TV Wall Hanging
153. Pack and Ship Business
154. Appliance Repair Business
155. Home Restoration/ Remodel Business
156. Graffiti Removal Business
157. Recycling Pick Up (in communities that do not have pick up from the city)
158. Asbestos Removal Business
159. Attic/ Basement Finishing
160. Brick Walkway/ Patio/ Outbuilding Construction
161. Deck Construction/ Maintenance
162. Purified Water Delivery
163. Electromagnetic Field Testing, Radiation. Radon Testing/ Inspection
164. Fire and Water Damage Repair/ Restoration
165. Sprinkler/ Pipe Installation
166. Real Estate Photography Business
167. Misting Systems Installation Business
168. Mobile Home/ Small Home Transportation
169. Odor Elimination and Control Business
170. Paper Shredding Business
171. Lead Testing/ Removal Business
172. Security Camera Installation Business
173. Silver Refurbishing Business
174. Sound Proofing Business
175. Stenciling and Artistic Painting for Children's Rooms/ Kitchens, etc
176. Stucco/ External Coating Contracting

177. Bed Bug/ Flea/ Lice Removal Business
178. Water Heater Repair/ Install Business
179. Water Well Find Location/ Drilling Business
180. Home Staging Business

For Kids/ Moms/ Teens/ Families

181. Baby Shoe Bronzing Service/ Concrete Keepsake Baby Handprint Service
182. In-Home Daycare
183. Babysitting Service
184. In-Home Preschool
185. Head Start Tutor for Babies/Toddlers/ Preschoolers
186. Tutor for Elementary, Jr. High. High School, and/ or College Students
187. Baby Bottle Sterilizing Service
188. Baby Food/ Supplies Delivery Service
189. Mother/ Infant Home Help Care Service
190. Child Chauffeur/ Accompaniment
191. Child Entertainment Service
192. Story Time and Snack Group
193. Youth Mentoring Service
194. College Financial Aid/ Scholarship Researcher
195. Lactation Consultant
196. Nanny Service
197. Childproofing Service/ Safety Consultant
198. Face Painting Stand
199. Classy Toddler Playtime Group (kids, moms dress up. moms served tea and cakes)
200. Graduation Photographer
201. College Application Consultant
202. Crowd Sourcing (bring talent to work)
203. Sports Activity Clinics (evening, Saturday, or Summer)
204. Petting Zoo
205. New Mom Meal Delivery (also for Seniors/ Disabled)
206. Paint Ball Field
207. Children's Museum
208. Pumpkin Patch/ Corn Maze/ Autumn Fun Place (Seasonal)
209. Grant Finder/ Writer for College Students
210. Afterschool Program
211. Mini Golf Course
212. Aptitude Test Prep and Practice Testing
213. Birth Announcement Service
214. A Camp
215. Educational Cooperative

216. Toddler Friendly Restaurant
217. Toddler Friendly Neighborhood Hangout, Tea, Coffee House
218. Genealogy Researcher
219. Child ID Service
220. Midwife
221. Toddler Friendly Contained Playground
222. Family/ Couple/ Child/ Baby Photography
223. Pregnancy Consulting/ Counseling
224. Child Railroad
225. Self Esteem Coach for Children/ Adults
226. Snow Making (for places where there is no snow)
227. 3D Ultrasounds
228. Child Friendly Dance Club
229. Skating Rink (Ice or Roller)
230. Teen Hangout
231. Children's Exercise Program Leader

Relaxation/ Exercise/ Body Related

232. Stress Management Consultant
233. Archery Field/ Range
234. Driving Range
235. Day Spa (manicures/ pedicures) (in home/ on location)
236. Personal Training
237. Private Golf/ Tennis Club
238. Sports Instruction (written or on field)
239. Tanning Booth Parlor
240. Recreation Center (indoor or outdoor)
241. Reflexology Practice
242. Massage Parlor (mobile or on location)
243. Weight Loss Coach/ Dietician
244. Acupuncture Clinic
245. Exercise Group Leader (aerobics, running, motivational)
246. Personal Healthy Food Chef
247. Yoga Instruction/ Studio
248. Meditation Leader/ Visualization Specialist
249. Healthy Living Consultant
250. Art/ Music Therapist
251. Beauty Salon (full service)
252. Electrolysis/ Waxing Service
253. Hair Cutting Only Salon
254. Ethnic Hair Salon (hair weaving, braiding, ethnic hair relaxation, straightening)
255. Life Skills/ Coaching
256. Ear Piercing Service
257. Body Piercing/ Tattoo Parlor
258. Drug Testing Service
259. Funeral Home
260. Henna Artist
261. Head Lice and Nit Removal (from person)
262. Fitness/ Health Club

Services

263. Telephone Answering Service/ Appointment Setting
264. Reminder Service/ Wake Up Call Service
265. Greeting Card Sending Service
266. Product Installation Service
267. Errand Running Service
268. Personal Assistant/ Virtual Assistant Business
269. Mobile Hand Car Wash
270. Business Plan Consulting
271. Product Photographer
272. Store Window Painting Service
273. Passport Headshot Photography
274. Office Support Service
275. Dating Agency
276. Silhouette Artist
277. Pen Pal Service (online and/or offline)
278. Video Taping Service
279. Computer Repair
280. Handwriting Analysis Service
281. Income Tax Preparation Service
282. Medical Billing Service/ Medical Recordkeeping Service
283. Windshield Repair
284. Towing Service
285. Auto Detailing
286. Building Appraisal Service
287. Parking Lot/ Road Line Painting
288. Social Media Specialist (set up, manage profiles, consulting, engaging customers)
289. Tech Support Service
290. Freelance Graphic Designing
291. Translation Service
292. Insurance Agency
293. Small Engine/ Appliance Repair
294. Personal Security/ Bodyguard/ Security
295. Fundraising Consultant/ Coordinator
296. Parking Lot Striping/ Painting
297. Web Design Consulting
298. Solar Energy/ Green Consultant
299. Junk Hauler (in cities without free pickup)

300. Affiliate Web Marketing
301. Rental Properties Repair and Cleanup
302. Auction House
303. Auto Repair Shop
304. Porcelain Repair
305. Boat Painting Service
306. Boat/Trailer Restoration
307. Bridal Gown Cleaning and Restoration
308. Internet Security Consultant
309. Business or Professional Club
310. Referral Service
311. Harvesting Business/ Pickers/ Farm Labor Contracting
312. Irrigation Ditch Contracting
313. Jewelry Repair
314. Mock Trial and Jury
315. Laundry Mat
316. Graphic Arts Consulting/ Logo Creation/ Book Art Design
317. Market Research Analysis Consulting
318. Public Relations Consulting
319. Mini-Storage
320. Non-Profit Agency
321. Notary Public (mobile or stationary)
322. Quality Control Consulting
323. Singles Organization/ Club
324. Web Site Hosting Service
325. Wrecking and Demolishing Business
326. Meat Slicing for Hunters/ Sausage Making
327. Creativity Consultant
328. Search Engine Optimization Consultant
329. Art Consultant
330. Mobile App Development Consulting
331. Day Care Sanitizing Business
332. Crime Scene Clean Up Business

Businesses Related to the Unemployed or People in Crisis

333. Repossession Service
334. Foreclosure Clean Up/ Repair
335. Bail Bond Lending with Interest
336. Cash Advance/ Loans Business
337. Lie Detection Service
338. Clean Up Janitorial Service (Hospitals, Crime Scenes, Work Sites)
339. Career Coach/ Career Consultant
340. Collections Agency
341. Abortion Alternatives Center
342. Adoption Agency
343. Employment Agency
344. Employment Agency (general or niche)
345. Temp Agency
346. 24 hour Suicide Watch Service
347. Paternity Testing Service
348. Missing Persons Organization
349. Gang Intervention Service
350. Crisis Center
351. Neighborhood Beautification Program

Seniors/ the Disabled/ Medical Related

352. Grocery Shopping Service
353. Adult Daycare/ Babysitting Service (respite for a caregiver, company for the disabled, seniors)
354. Senior/ Disabled Shuttle/ Taxi Service
355. Elder Employment Agency
356. Disabled Employment Agency
357. Senior Consignment Store
358. Email/ Computer Lessons for Seniors
359. Entertainment Service for the Homebound
360. Wheel Chair Repair
361. Home Meal Delivery (also see kids/ moms)
362. Assisted Living Facility
363. Rest Home/ Nursing Home
364. Start a Bingo Hall
365. Start a Support Group
366. Air-Ambulance Service for Remote Locations
367. Naturopathic Dr.
368. Alzheimer's Care Facility
369. Recovery Care Business
370. Companion for Elderly/ Disabled
371. Hypnotherapist
372. Music Therapy Business
373. Pain Coach
374. Relaxation Therapist
375. Disability Assistance/ Advocacy Association
376. Respiratory Therapist
377. School for the Deaf/ Blind
378. School for the Physically Challenged
379. Sleep Disorder Clinic
380. Ultrasound/ Medical Imaging
381. Animal Care/ House Care for the Disabled/ Post Op

Adventure/ Travel/ Tourism Related Businesses

382. Hot Air Balloon Rides
383. Parasailing Trips
384. Scuba diving Trips
385. Cross Country Skiing Trips
386. Snorkel Trips
387. Guided Hikes (meals/ snacks included)
388. Local Tour Guide/ Bus Tours/ Van Tours/ Walking Tours/ Segway Tours
389. Private Investigator
390. Courier/ Hand Delivery Service
391. Guided Travel Host (international or long distance)
392. Helicopter Tours
393. Campground (rent out spaces)
394. RV Park
395. Air Boat Tours/ Boat Tours
396. Air Sightseeing Tours/ Charters
397. Airline
398. Archeological Digging Business
399. ATV Tours
400. Bike Tours (mountain, city, or countryside)
401. Boat Charters
402. Interisland Ferry
403. Interisland Freight Service
404. Gold Panning/ Ghost Town/ Old West Tourist Instruction
405. Hang Gliding Business
406. Traditional Small Village/ Town with Activities
407. Expeditions (hunting, photographic, camping, etc)
408. Lake Sea Resort/ Hotel/ Cabin Rentals
409. Observatory
410. Specialty Resort
411. Adventure Outfitters/ Tours and Guides (desert, wilderness, safari)
412. Paint Ball Facility (outdoor)
413. Rustic/ Vintage Tea Service/ Picnic Meal Setup in Remote or Outdoor Location
414. Rafting Trips/ Tours
415. Shooting Range/ Target Practice Range
416. Ropes/ Obstacle Course

417. Sailing Tours/ Charters
418. Ski Resort/ Tours
419. Water Park/ Slides
420. Water Ski Instruction/ Trips
421. Zoo
422. Field Data Research Gatherer
423. Local Taxi/ Car Service
424. Skywriting/ Banner Service
425. Bicycle Delivery/ Currier Service (large city)
426. International Money Exchange
427. Outsourcing Business (go between)
428. Museum
429. Dormitory/ Youth Hostel
430. Bed and Breakfast (can start out of spare room or out building)
431. Trail Riding Expeditions (horse back)
432. Toiletry/ Food/ Suitcase/ Walking Shoe Delivery for Travelers

Pets/ Animals/ Farm Related Businesses

433. Aquarium Maintenance Service
434. Pet Taxi Service
435. Dog Walking Service
436. Pet Babysitting Service
437. Pooper Scooper Service
438. Dog Entertainer Service
439. Mobile Dog/ Cat Feeder and Care Service (for people out of town or at work)
440. Mobile Pet Grooming Service
441. Breeder (horse, dog, rare cat, etc)
442. Petting Zoo
443. Pet Psychologist
444. Rent a Pet (horse, dog, etc)
445. Dog Trainer (also under teaching)
446. Pet Cemetery (can include selling burial plots, coffins, headstones, memorials, and performing funeral services)
447. Door to Door Pony Rides and Photography of Children on the Pony/ Tiny Horse
448. Animal Kennel
449. Pet Shop
450. Horse Shoeing
451. Animal Therapy
452. Animal Trapping Business
453. Boarding Stables
454. Butterfly Hatchery
455. Horse and Carriage Rides
456. Raise and Sell Cattle
457. Raise and Sell Chickens
458. Raise Chickens to sell Eggs
459. Herb Farm
460. Flower Farm
461. Fish/ Shrimp Hatchery
462. U Pick Farm
463. CSA Farm
464. Sell Produce to Farmer's Markets
465. Llama/ Alpaca Farm
466. Become a Fisherman, Sell Catches
467. Plant/ Tree Nursery

468. Organic Farm
469. Pet Loss Counselor
470. Taxidermist
471. Horse Trail Rides (also on Travel)
472. Pet Hotel
473. Dove Releases
474. Beekeeping/ Honey Production

Things/ Places You Can Rent Out

475. Musical Instruments
476. City Bikes/ Racing Bikes/ Mountain Bikes
477. A Recording Studio
478. Costumes
479. Wedding Dresses
480. Boats/ Yachts
481. Formal Dresses/ Evening Gowns
482. Waterslides/ Carnival Dunk Tanks/ Inflatable Play Equipment
483. Outdoor Gear/ Camping Supplies
484. Small Trailers/ Campers
485. Furniture/ Computers (possible rent to own)
486. Luxury Accessories (purses, shoes, clothes, hair pieces)
487. Movies/ Video Games
488. Spare Room Storage/ Storage Facility/ Mini-Storage
489. Spare Room Boarding House
490. Beach Equipment (kites, snorkels, fins, dive equipment)
491. Sports Equipment
492. Human Billboard Rentals
493. Car Wrapping Service (sell advertising space on cars)
494. Campsite Space Rental
495. Party Bus Rental with Driver
496. Start a Farmer's Market (rent out stalls)
497. Start a Flea Market (rent out stalls)
498. Tuxedo Rentals
499. Car Rental Agency
500. Baby Furniture Rental
501. Cabin/ Chalet/ Cottage Vacation Rentals
502. Bone China/ Glassware/ Tea Sets/ Crystal/ Formal Dinner Party Accessory Rentals
503. Classroom Equipment (microscopes, models, dioramas, etc)
504. Holiday Front Yard Display Rentals
505. Jet Ski Rentals
506. Karaoke Machine/ Microphones/ Speakers/ Performance Equipment Rentals
507. Golf Cart Rentals
508. Office and Loft Building Rental or Real Estate Agency

509. Piano Rentals
510. Port a Potty Rentals
511. RV Rentals
512. RV Storage Space Rentals
513. Snow Mobile Rentals
514. Hot Tub/ Spa Rentals (possible rent to own)
515. Start an Art Consignment Store (rent out space)
516. Event Prop Rentals (arbors, trellises, tents, etc)
517. Maternity Clothes/ Children's Clothing Rentals
518. Houses/ Residences/ Condos/ Apartments/ Cabin Rentals

Classes You Can Teach

You could turn many of these into a school or classes to teach yourself and/ or have others teach. Many of these can also be taught at parties.

519. Etiquette for Children/ Adults
520. Poetry (different types of, how to create self published books, marketing, how to get published by an established magazine/ book publisher)
521. Classy Classes (Such as tea service)
522. Hat Decoration
523. Day Basket Design/ Decorating
524. Jewelry Design/ Making
525. Dress Design
526. Painting/ Art
527. Cooking School
528. Paper Doll Making
529. Flower Arranging
530. A Foreign Language You Speak/ Hire a Native Speaker to Teach
531. Cake/ Cupcake Design
532. Conversation Skills
533. Photography Techniques
534. Sewing/ Cross Stitching
535. Aerobics
536. Driving to New Drivers
537. Tutoring
538. Juggling
539. Tarot Card Reading
540. Mom and Tot First Preschool for 2-3 year olds
541. Other Mom and Tot Classes
542. Sign Language for New Moms
543. Survival Skills for Local Outdoor Area
544. Local History/ History of Your Interests
545. Swimming Lessons
546. Origami
547. Child Behavior Management/ Empathy Classes for Parents
548. Computer Instruction (basic e-mail for seniors program, general instruction, programming, etc)

549. Crochet/ Knitting/ Sewing
550. Musical Instrument Lessons
551. Voice Lessons
552. Puppet Creation/ Performance
553. Life Skills Coaching
554. Life Skills Teaching People to be Life Skills Coaches
555. Create Course Books and Teach Classes on Subjects Knowledgeable to You
556. Career Counseling Classes
557. Entrepreneurship for Kids
558. Self-Defense Classes
559. Baby Sign Language
560. Teach a Class for Something You are Certified in
561. Acting
562. Your Favorite Academic Niche (biology, a culture, zoology, etc)
563. Astrology/ Astronomy
564. Auto Mechanic School
565. Dance Classes/ School
566. Bartending Class/ School
567. Baton Twirling
568. Beauty School
569. Religious Study School (correspondence or in person)
570. Boxing
571. Karate/ Shiatsu
572. Bronzing collectables (baby shoes, etc)
573. Cheerleading/ Color Guard
574. Chess
575. Backgammon
576. Mancala
577. Circus Act School
578. Teach CPR
579. Court Reporting School
580. English as a Second Language
581. Fencing
582. Hunting
583. Hypnosis
584. Locksmith
585. Macramé

586. Martial Arts
587. Medical/ Office Secretarial School
588. Meditation/ Yoga/ Relaxation
589. Modeling Classes/ School (can open along with an agency)
590. Start a Montessori School
591. Motivation/ Self Improvement Classes
592. Parasailing
593. Piano
594. Private Detective School
595. Public Speaking
596. Reading Improvement Instruction
597. Scholarship/ Grant Finding Instruction
598. Surfing Lessons/ Surf School
599. Silhouette Art
600. Real Estate School
601. Sailing School
602. Sales
603. Scuba
604. Secretarial School
605. Teaching the Art of Selling
606. Scuba School
607. Skydiving School
608. Language School for Children
609. Spinning/ Weaving/ Ancient Arts Classes
610. Square Dance
611. Stained Glass Making
612. Paper Weight Painting for Kids
613. Stress Management
614. Tennis
615. Wrestling
616. Writing
617. Yoga
618. Genealogy Research
619. Cooking Classes/ Cooking Classes for Kids
620. Collectables Research

Selling Businesses

621. Buy and Relist Better on Ebay
622. Sell Own Stuff on Ebay (continue by selling stuff for others and taking a percentage of the sale)
623. Sell Homemade Crafts (at fairs, Etsy, Ebay, yard sales, on own web site)
624. Market a Local Product Nationally
625. Home Party Craft Sales
626. Direct Selling Home Parties of Merchandise Direct from Manufacturers
627. Door to Door Sales of Your Favorite or Homemade Goods
628. Collectables Searcher/ Dealer
629. Coin Dealer or Dealer of your Favorite Hobby
630. Consignment Shop/ Children's Clothing/ Elderly Clothing/ Maternity/ Other Niche 2nd Hand Sales
631. Weekly Yard Sales
632. Buy in Bulk, Resell
633. Rare Book Broker
634. Club Membership Website or Association with Dues
635. Of the Month Club Website
636. Kiosk Selling Merchandise in High Traffic Areas
637. Real Estate (start small/ affordable properties, fix up property, sell)
638. Used CD Resell Shop (online and off)
639. Fix Up and Sell Cars/ Old Boats/ Trailers
640. Entertainment Memorabilia
641. Art/ Painting Live Portraits
642. Pawn Shop
643. Online Drop Shipping Retailer
644. Sell Your Photos to a Stock Photo Agency/ Sell Prints
645. Sell Flower Arrangements/ Florist
646. Start a Call Center
647. Start an Insurance Agency
648. Sell Burial Insurance
649. Sell Dance Clothing/ Tutus/ Whimsical Play Clothes for Preschoolers or Early Elementary School Students
650. Start a Rural General Store
651. Become a Middle Man for Drop Shipping
652. Start a Ethnic Gift/ Book Shop/ Clothing Store

653. Resell Underpriced Land
654. Start an Antique Store (offline and/or online)
655. Metaphysical Store (with fortune telling services)
656. Military Whole Sale (great for rural area)
657. Golf Carts/ Moped Sales
658. Online Store
659. Buy and Sell Handmade Items such as Quilts
660. Start a Religious Goods Store
661. Start a Rent to Own Business
662. Start an Unknown Purchase Store (example sell a box of unknown stuff for 10 dollars)
663. Video Game/ DVD Resells
664. Scrap Metal Scavenging to Local Scrappers
665. Sell hair extensions at home "try on" parties

Things You Can Make and Sell

666. Baby Burp Cloths
667. Patchwork Quilts
668. Gift Baskets
669. Paintings (landscapes, portraits, etc)
670. Self Published Books/ Booklets (local history, poetry, how to handbooks, stories, non-fiction)
671. Jewelry
672. Crochet/ Knit Items (scarves, etc)
673. Sewed Items (clothes, dolls, blankets, etc)
674. Greeting Cards
675. Accessories (especially for little girls...big bows, beautiful/ flowery hats, flowers, purses etc or for women...handbag line, hair accessories, hats)
676. Baby Name Stenciled Letters for a Child's Room
677. Junk/ Up cycled Sculptures
678. Up cycled Clothing
679. Small Children's Clothing (especially little girl's dresses, tutus)
680. Puppets
681. Ice Sculptures for Special Occasions
682. Dog Houses
683. Pet Toys
684. Mother/ Daughter Matching Clothing/ Accessories
685. Professional Yard Sale Sign Creation and Installation
686. Santa Letters for Kids
687. Pottery
688. Lucky Charms (rabbit's feet, horse shoes, 4 leaf clovers that are preserved or pressed)
689. Professionally Frame and Sell Your own Landscape Photos
690. Board Games
691. Balloon/ Flower Arrangements
692. Tea/ Formal Dinner Napkins/ Table Cloths/ Crochet Doilies/ Other Linens
693. Candy Grams
694. Start a Fashion Label
695. Homemade Soaps
696. Organic Lotions with All Natural Ingredients
697. Draperies

698. Items with Electronic Embroidery or Monogrammed
699. Decked Out Golf Carts for Teens
700. Hand Blown Glass
701. Furniture Refurbishing and Reselling/ Hand Painted
702. Macramé Items
703. Native/ Natural Arts (dream catchers, chemical free clothing, etc)
704. Natural/ Chemical Free Perfume/ Cologne Manufacturing
705. Ship Building and Selling
706. Wedding Favors
707. Wedding Centerpieces
708. Wood Carving
709. Christmas Decorations/ Ornaments
710. Play date Fun Packs (pre planned activities for play dates in a box or bag)
711. Footwear/ Sandals
712. Comfortable and Beautiful Summer Dresses
713. Timeless Clothing
714. Affiliate Marketing Website (make your own website and sell for others eBooks, advertisements, other's products, services and get commission)

Food/ Drink Related Businesses

715. Tea House/ Shop
716. Picnic Lunches to Go
717. Coffee House
718. Concession Stand
719. Sidewalk Café (with or without theme)
720. Deli
721. Supper Delivery Club
722. Paying Dinner Parties
723. Roaming Food Truck (use social media for locations)
724. Cookouts
725. Breakfast in Bed Service
726. Breakfast/ Lunch/ Dinner/ Tea in the Bush
727. Winery/ Wine Making/ Tasting
728. Cake Decorating/ Delivery
729. Healthy Brown Bag Lunch Sales
730. Something Obscure in a Progressive Area
731. Ice Cream Truck
732. Mobile Café/ Shop/ Restaurant
733. Food Stand/ Cart/ Restaurant
734. Ethnic Grocery Store
735. Specialty Grocery Store
736. Basics Grocery Store
737. Health Food Grocery Store
738. Kosher Grocery Store
739. Catering Business
740. Dehydrated Food Manufacturing/ Sales
741. Food Manufacturing/ Sales
742. Make and Sell Tamales
743. Salad Dressing/ Sauce Manufacturing/ Sales
744. Microbrewery/ Beer Production
745. Snow Cone Stand
746. Ethnic or Specialty Bakery

Types of Restaurant Businesses You can Start

747. American Food/ Grill/ Bar and Grill
748. Kosher or Ethnic Jewish Food
749. French (If you have chosen an ethnicity of food that you enjoy. Consider then researching the different types of restaurant establishments from that country or ethnicity. You might start a new restaurant trend!)
- Brasserie
- Bouchon
- Café
- Café Gourmand
- Bistrot
- Traditional Auberge
- Auberge du Terroir
- Bouvette
- Creperie
- Ferme-Auberge
- Rotisserie
- Salon du The
- Taverne
- Estaminet
- French Fusion
- Chocolatier
- Traiteur
- Le Restaurant
750. Start a New Ethnic Restaurant Trend
    1. Pick Your Favorite Country or Ethnicity
    2. Google types of Restaurants
    3. Research types of Food Served
    4. Seek Out to Experience These Foods
    5. Decorate your Restaurant in Excess According to that Country or Culture
    6. Learn to Cook These Foods or Hire Someone who Knows How
751. Mexican/ Cantina
752. Caribbean Restaurant
753. Cuban Restaurant
754. Polish Restaurant

755. Chinese/ Asian Restaurant
756. BBQ Restaurant Stationary
757. Chuck wagon BBQ
758. Steakhouse
759. Dinner Train
760. Bridge Restaurant
761. Health Food Restaurant
762. Themed Restaurant
763. Pop Up Restaurant (use social media)
764. Tower Restaurant
765. Restaurant on a Boat
766. Restaurant on a Plane
767. Dinner Theater (for adults or children)
768. Cafeteria
769. Vegetarian Restaurant
770. Drive In Restaurant
771. Doughnut Shop
772. Fast Food Restaurant
773. Seafood Restaurant/ or Fish and Chips Restaurant
774. Ice Cream Parlor/ Root Beer Float Parlor
775. Pizza Parlor
776. Sandwich Shop
777. Buffet
778. Hotel/ Restaurant
779. Regional Theme Restaurant (Midwestern Food/ Southern Food/ etc)
780. Diner
781. Breakfast Establishment
782. Holiday Meal Restaurant Theme
783. Delicatessen/ Deli
784. Italian Restaurant
785. Truck Stop Restaurant
786. Snack Bar
787. Irish Restaurant/ Pub/ Brewery
788. Fine Dining/ White Tablecloth
789. Family Style Restaurant
790. Indian Restaurant
791. Mongolian Stir Fry Restaurant
792. Destination Restaurant/ With Attraction(s)

793. Fondue/ Cook Your Own Food Restaurant
794. Ethiopian Restaurant/ African Restaurant
795. Restaurant with a DJ/ Dance Floor
796. Cabin Restaurant
797. Spanish Restaurant
798. Greek Restaurant
799. Thai Restaurant

Types of Bars You Can Open

800. Wine Bar
801. Basic Traditional Bar (with or without theme)
802. Piano Bar
803. Dive Bar
804. Oyster Bar
805. Seafood Bar (with shrimp cocktails, clam chowders, cold sea foods, etc)

Non-Profits and Societies You Can Start.

Make money from government grants and subsidies, donations, selling of products, sponsors, fund raising events, etc

As with starting any small business, be sure to research the rules and laws of running a Non-Profit or Society in your Community, City, County, State, and Country before getting started. Tax payment, laws, how to collect your paycheck, and much more are different than regular businesses.

806. Help Feed Poor Children/ Disabled/ Mothers with Young Children/ Adults in Far off Places of Little Opportunity or in the US
807. Help Preserve Something or Someplace
808. Religious Group or Organization
809. Promoting Safety to the Public (get the word out for a cause/ prevent or help)
810. Any Organization that Helps Create a Sense of Community or Place
811. Help People Learn Something (a foreign language, job skills, to read, etc)
812. Help Animals (animal shelters/ animal rights organization)
813. Help the Elderly
814. Advocacy for a Group or Cause
815. Start a Community Library
816. Start a Homeless Shelter
817. Start a Museum
818. Start a Theater
819. Start a Hospital
820. Start a School/ College
821. Start an Organization for Environmental Protection
822. Human Rights Advocacy Organization
823. A Security Organization
824. Organization that Aids the Unemployed/ Homeless/ Poor
825. Cemetery
826. Organization that Promotes Volunteering
827. Historical Society
828. Vocational School
829. Community Beautification Organization
830. Ethnic/ Gender Studies Organizations
831. Helping people with Addictions/ Mental Disorders
832. Helping people with a Specific Health Problem Get Access to Current Research and Support

833. Medical Research
834. Crime/ Legal Related Organization
835. Disaster Preparedness Organization
836. Organization Promoting Intercultural/ Interreligious Understanding
837. Helping Promote Understanding for The Disabled/ Group/ Religious Group/ Ethnic Group/ The Poor
838. Civil Rights Organization
839. Any Organization that Helps the Public as a Whole
840. Religious Promotion/ Proselytizing/ Study Organization
841. An Organization that Helps Children
842. An Organization that Helps Battered Women
843. An Organization that Promotes an Educational Idea
844. A Society that Promotes the Culture of an Ethnic or Religious Group
845. A Society that Promotes an Idea
846. Any other Group/ Organization that forms for a Mission to Help or Preserve

Start a Club (Collect Regular Dues, Hold Fundraisers)

847. Language Club
848. Culture Club
849. Travel Club
850. Hobby Club
851. Volunteer/ Service Club
852. Tea/ Luncheon Club
853. Sports Club/ League
854. Women's Club
855. Religious Club
856. Book Club
857. Social Club
858. Time Period Reenactment Club
859. Craft Club
860. Children's Club
861. Party/ Event Club
862. Outdoor Recreation Club
863. Board Game Club
864. Writing Club (Fiction, Poetry, etc.)
865. Pot Luck Cooking Club
866. Walking Club
867. Exercise Club
868. Adventure Club (planned adventure sports trips)
869. Single's Club
870. Reading Club/ Group

General Tips for Success
Before You Get Started

1. Make sure there is a market for your product and/or service in your local area or online if you are conducting business there. Conduct market research before you get started if you are unsure.
2. Always stay organized to find everything quickly when you need it. Whether for a sale or for your own sanity.
3. Keep costs as low as possible without sacrificing quality.
4. Add lots of extra touches and make sure clients or customers will get feelings of respect and importance when doing business with you.
5. Have lots of background knowledge about your business. Do extra research before going into business to make sure you have all the necessary skills, degrees/ certifications, financial start up costs, and necessary permits to conduct your choice business in your area. Make sure you check with a local business attorney to make sure you are running your business legally in your area. Don't be discouraged, many of the businesses in this book require no certifications/ skills.
6. Always pay your taxes and pay them on time. Research what the tax rates are in your country, state, county, city, community for charging your customers and for yourself to pay. Research how you will pay and where to pay to before getting started.
7. Always conduct your business honestly and ethically.
8. Be unique to stand out.
9. Consider the words you use in your advertising. The modern human mind is attracted to words such as "free" and "for a limited time." These words and many more that speak to the customer's best interest or peak the customer's excitement easily attract

attention. Make your advertising exciting and beneficial to the customer.

10. Always screen employees (do a full background check) if you hire them to have contact with children, access to money, or to have access to a client's home.

11. Keep start up costs as low as possible. If you have to take out a second mortgage, you could lose everything if your business fails. This is most likely not the right business for you at this time. Start small and build from the ground up.

12. Pick a business that caters to a "niche" or specialty market and advertise in places where your specific potential clientele might be exposed to or might congregate.

13. Don't ever give up if your heart is in it just change up your type of advertising, products, etc.

14. Purchase insurance

15. If you have one, keep your day job until your business takes off. Do not rely on the success of your new business until you notice over a long period of time that it is successful and is consistently bringing in revenue.

16. Keep an eye out for my next book that will list for you over 230 ways to advertise. You'll never wonder how you can reach more people or how you should be advertising. Great for the new small business/ organization owner or the seasoned owner who has run out of ideas.

Keep updated at: http://www.SaraMartinAuthor.com

Free and Inexpensive Resources for New and/or Frugal Business Owners

Free Business Management Information from A-Z
http://managementhelp.org

Government Grant Information and Much More
US Small Business Administration
http://www.sba.gov

Branding Services
http://www.zazzle.com
http://www.branders.com
http://www.cafepress.com

Free Websites and blogs
http://www.wordpress.com
http://www.blogger.com
http://www.weebly.com
http://www.webs.com
http://www.urblogz.com
http://www.1freecart.com
http://www.vstore.ca
http://www.angelfire.com
http://www.tripod.com
http://www.freewebsites.com
http://www.yola.com
http://www.webplusshop.com
http://www.bravenet.com
http://www.googlesites.com

A Wealth of Stock Photo Web Sites for Your Every Need, Many Free!
http://smallbiztrends.com/2011/01/image-sites-small-business.html

Free E-Mail
http://www.gmail.com
http://www.yahoo.com
http://www.outlook.com (formerly hotmail)

Free Brochure Maker
http://www.mybrochuremaker.com

Free Business Card Maker and More
http://www.printfree.com
http://www.nashua.com/tmplts.html (need Microsoft Word or
Works)
http://www.templates4cards.com

Free Printable Certificates
http://www.freeprintablecertificates.net

Free Graphics Generator
http://www.cooltext.com

Free Mentoring
From Retired Executives
http://www.score.org
From Your Local Small Business Development Center
http://www.sba.gov (click on "Local Assistance")

Free Office Furniture
http://www.craigslist.com
http://www.freecycle.com

**Share Power Point Presentations Online, Convert PowerPoint to
Video, and Broadcast PowerPoint Presentations Live**
http://www.authorstream.com

Free Conference Calling
http://www.freeconferencecall.com
http://www.groupme.com
http://www.wiggio.com
http://www.fring.com

Free Logo Makers
http://www.logomaker.com
http://www.logosnap.com
http://www.allfreelogos.com

Free Boxes for Mailing (free Priority Mail boxes available at most post offices for easy pick up)
http://www.usps.com

Conduct Surveys
http://www.surveymonkey.com

500 Free Business Plan Samples for a Variety of Businesses AND How To Write a Business Plan
http://www.bplans.com

Chat Live With Customers on Your Website for Free
http://www.livehelpengine.com

Free Web Submission (your URL will be submitted to over 1,600 web sites to be featured for free)
http://www.pingmyurl.com

Free Image Hosting (for Ebay auctions, etc)
http://www.thefreesite.com/Free_Image_Hosting/

Buy Domain Name(s)
http://www.godaddy.com

Free Stuff for Webmasters (guest books, counters, message boards, site promotion services, page counters, polls, easy interactive forms, days to go countdowns, and more)
http://www.thefreesite.com/Webmaster_Freebies